DOWN TO EARTH

AN EASY GUIDE TO GROWING YOUR OWN VEGETABLES SUCCESSFULLY

Madeleine Cardozo

First published in Great Britain by

Haxnicks Ltd
Beaumont Business Estate
Mere
Wiltshire
BA12 6BT

www.haxnicks.co.uk

ISBN: 978-0-9566379-0-1

Photography: Madeleine Cardozo
Book design: Jaz Wiseman

Printed and bound in England by Butler Tanner & Dennis, Frome, Somerset.

Acknowledgements:
I would like to thank in particular my husband Damian for his encouragement and support, my children Tilly, Jack, Lali, Louis, Orlando and Bruno for their help and advice on my photography and recipes. My fellow gardeners for their help and advice, Dom and Arabella Parish, Anna and James Mackain Bremner, Pepi Hughes, Chlöe Cardozo and Trish Scott Bolton, Mitch Earl, Sophie, Bamber and Leo Mauleverer, Lucy Irwin, Thingy Compton, Alex Head, Vicky Standing and of course Jaz Wiseman.

Contents

 Easy   Not So Easy    Difficult

In The Beginning

I am not quite sure where to begin, but it's definitely way after Adam and Eve. In fact I think that I will start with something like the autumn. Remember that nothing I write has to be taken literally. If you have left something a little late like transplanting a plant when it is more than 7cm (3") tall, think logically and you will be fine. Each gardener will end up doing their own thing according to how organised or disorganised they are. In this book I am sharing with you my knowledge, my own experiences and how it works for me. One of my strong beliefs is deciding what you want to do and giving it a go – I still don't have any kiwi fruit on my kiwi trees!

There is nothing like eating your own home grown produce. For the first couple of years you may think that financially it doesn't make sense, but as you become more experienced it can save you money. Quite apart from the benefits of how good gardening is for your health, there is the satisfaction, relaxation, exercise and having an excuse to be out in the fresh air.

It is well worth doing your homework and reading a few gardening magazines or books, relating to what you want to do in your garden. This can provide many shortcuts and much better results.

So in the autumn...

In November I like to clear everything, except my winter vegetables and get ready for the winter months.

Your summer crops from the patch should have died a death by now and need to be removed, don't worry if you leave a few roots as you can dig them in and they will rot down leaving a few extra nutrients. When the soil is not too wet, dig up your entire patch turning over the soil and forking it through. Add 5 - 7cm (2" - 3") thick of well rotted manure or compost. This acts as a natural fertiliser and improves the quality of your soil immensely; when in doubt pile it on! In fact I use manure all over my garden, on the raspberries, roses, everywhere. My crops can be twice the size given a good dollop of manure. If you don't have access to something like manure from horses, chickens or cows, you can buy it in the garden centres either in sacks, liquids or pellet versions. Chicken manure is particularly high in nutrients, but don't use too much as it will also increase soil acidity. You can even use human manure, but for some reason the idea doesn't seem that appealing, not to mention transporting it to your vegetable patch - can't think why. Leave your patch like this until the spring.

Looking After Your Patch

Most gardeners keep their vegetable patch in the same place every year – this is normal. But if you plant and grow the same old stuff in the same old place year in and year out, not adding any compost etc, you will be a very disappointed gardener. Which is why you a) **add compost** b) **rotate your crops** and c) **weed**.

My cousin once said, when I asked her if I should put more compost onto my patch 'if you've got it flaunt it.' But remember that root vegetables don't like manure as it makes them unusual shapes, so no manure where you are going to plant your carrots, parsnips, swedes, etc.

Four year rotations are perhaps the easiest, I know this sounds like a long time and very complicated but you only have to start with the 1st year to get going, anyhow all this means is dividing your patch up into four parts, and changing them round every year say going clockwise or something. Here are the four groups for you to rotate in, legumes (e.g. peas or beans), brassicas (e.g. cauliflower or broccoli) roots and onions (e.g. beetroot or spring onions) and lastly the Solanaceae family (tomatoes and potatoes for the likes of you and me) Salads and the courgette family are very versatile and you can plant these anywhere.

If you want to have a three year rotation patch, I suggest planting your potatoes and tomatoes in patio planters or some old car tyres. I find that growing potatoes and tomatoes in patio planters is more successful on the whole, than planting them into the ground.

Weeding is very important especially when the plants are young and not yet established. It is best to weed around the plants until the wanted plant has dominated the area and is sucking up all the goodness from the ground around leaving very little for the weeds.

The Importance of Your Soil

This may sound fussy, but once you have sorted out the earth that you are to plant in, the growing becomes more successful and easier. Different areas in the country have different qualities; here are the three main types of soils: Clay, Loamy and Sandy.

Clay	Loam	Sand
Water retentive and hard to dig	A mix of silt and sand	Free draining
Very fine particles	This is your heart's desire	Large particles
Add lots of compost sand and manure	Make sure it also has nutrients in from composts	Add lots of compost and manure
		Needs more watering

When you grow plants they need nutrients from the soil, once you have used up the nutrients they will need to be replaced with compost or some other kind of fertiliser like manure.

In other words just add a good supply of compost or well rotted manure to your vegetable patch and you will be OK. If your soil is very full of clay remove the top soil then add some sand or grit to improve drainage and then replace your topsoil and mix in some compost. It seems hard but once you have it sussed you will be well rewarded.

Companion Planting

Companion planting means that you plant crops or flowers next to certain other crops or flowers to protect them from being invaded by nasty damaging creatures such as the cabbage white butterfly or aphids and flea beetles. Companion plants can also attract the right kind of pollinating insects. Here is a small list of easy things to grow that should make a difference to the quality of your crops.

Companion Plant	Crop	How It Helps
Onion family	Most vegetables, especially carrots	Overpowering scent, deters pests
Basil	Tomatoes and aubergines	Attracts Aphids, leaving crops un-invaded
Coriander	Most vegetables	Attracts bees and repels aphids and carrot fly
Marigolds	Most vegetables	Deters nematodes, slugs and wireworms
Mint	Cabbages, tomatoes and radishes	Deters flies, aphids and flea beetles
Nasturtiums	Brassicas (cabbages) and lettuces	Attracts cabbage whites away from crops
Oregano	Brassicas	Repels cabbage whites and attracts insects
Rosemary	Legumes, brassicas and carrots	Repels cabbage whites and attracts insects
Sage	Brassicas, carrots and radishes	Repels cabbage moth, carrot fly and beetles
Thyme	Most vegetables	Deters pests

Compost

Explanation

Every gardener should have some kind of compost heap, no matter how small the garden. We have so much kitchen waste – teabags, eggshells, rotten lettuce leaves as well as waste from the garden, dead leaves, grass cuttings, annual weeds... so why not use it and put it back into the earth.

Composting can take anything between two months and one year. It all depends on the ingredients, how often you turn the compost over and how bulky the compost is when you add it. There are two groups for your compost, quite logical really, the *Greens* and the *Browns*.

Greens	*Browns*
Grass cuttings	Straw and hay
Annual weeds (not perennials)	Twigs and leaves
Tea Bags	Cardboard and paper
Manure	Hedge and tree clippings
Diluted urine	Old bedding plants

The idea is to have fairly equal amounts of greens and browns, turn the compost between once a week and once a month to air it. This can mean transferring it from one heap to an adjacent heap.

Don't do what I did for years which was to have my heap under some trees in a sheltered spot, where no rain could get to it. I had to water it – boring!

Obviously the smaller your ingredients the faster your compost will decompose. Some people like to chop it up with a shredder, lawnmower or shears. I can't be bothered and just keep piling it on and mixing it.

Don't throw any foods onto your compost heap that the rats or foxes might like, such as meat cheese, bread etc. Cat litters and dog poo can encourage unwanted parasites, yuck. Also watch out for weeds with seeds like doc leaves, you don't want to lay them neatly across your vegetable patch ready to grow in the spring. Let them rot separately.

Main Points:

1. Equal amounts of greens and browns.
2. Have two or even better three heaps next to each other
3. Mix each heap up between once and four times a month
4. Make sure it is moist

Staggered Planting

Sowing your seeds in stages is a good way of staggering your harvest. For example lettuces can take 6 - 8 weeks between the time of sowing and cutting, but after two or three weeks of being perfect, they are ready to bolt. Now you don't want to plant a pack of 300 seeds all at once and have say 250 lettuces growing altogether. You will only have space for some and if there are too many you may not have time to eat them before they bolt. The solution: only plant about 25 seeds every other week and then you will have a constant flow of lettuces throughout the summer. This also means that one pack of seeds can last all season. You can do this with other vegetables too, maybe just have say two or three sowings of peas, carrots, courgettes, endive, radishes... instead of one. Planting in stages is only meant for the quicker growing vegetable. Slower vegetables such as tomatoes and sweet corn you sow only once.

You can also buy several varieties of vegetables such as leeks, an early, mid season or late variety, depending when you want to plant them or harvest them. In this case you would have to buy three different packets of seeds. Maybe start with a mid-range one and when you have more confidence try others.

A Rough Guide of What To Do And When To Do It In Your Vegetable Patch

January
Sow. Early seeds indoors such as tomatoes and broad beans, in late January.
Jobs. Dump manure onto your patch and mix it in if you haven't already done this. Cover your existing plants such as rhubarb and raspberries with manure.
Harvest. Any remaining cabbages, kale or brussels sprouts.

February
Sow. A few more seeds indoors such as asparagus, peppers, chillies, cabbages, cauliflowers, onions, leeks and lettuces. Plant garlic sets in cold weather.
Jobs. Break down earth by digging or rotavating, dig in manure and rake it over. Cover your strawberries with cloches or tunnels. Chit your seed potatoes. If you are forcing rhubarb cover it now under a bucket or rhubarb forcer.

March
Sow. Seeds indoors such as aubergines, brussels sprouts, celery, cucumbers, fennel, kale, lettuces, melons, nasturtiums, marigolds, peas and rocket.
Sow. Seeds directly outdoors such as, onion (sets), parsnips, potatoes, spinach, rhubarb (crowns), and strawberry (plants).
Jobs. Hoe any weeds that pop up in your vegetable patch.

April
Sow. Seeds indoors such as climbing and dwarf beans, courgettes and endives.
Sow. Seeds directly outdoors such as beetroot, carrots, swedes, asparagus (crowns) and late potatoes.
Jobs. Protect any seedlings with cloches and slug deterrents. Place straw under strawberries to protect them from the cold and wet.

May
Sow. 2nd batches of seeds such as lettuce, beans , carrots, cabbages, peas...
Jobs. Harden off and plant out crops to go under poly tunnels. Protect all soft fruits from birds by covering with netting of some sort. Pinch out tips of broad beans and extra stems from tomatoes. Get rid of unwanted weeds.
Harvest. Asparagus, rhubarb, strawberries, and any lettuces.

June

Sow. Directly outdoors another batch of lettuce, radishes, rocket...

Jobs. Lots of planting out to do in June, empty most of your windowsill and greenhouse pots. Thin out any surplus plants such as carrots and beetroot. Tie tomatoes, peas and beans to canes or plant supports. If hot remove poly tunnels and replace with netting if necessary.

Harvest. Soft fruits, broad beans, peas, lettuces, more asparagus. Pick beetroot leaves for salads.

July

Sow. Lots of salady things, rocket, lettuce, endives...

Jobs. Plant out the last of your greenhouse/windowsill plants. Make sure the plants are all watered well and regularly, during the evening is best. Peg down the strawberry runners to raise new strawberry plants. Watch out for all pests, squish or relocate caterpillars, put down slug deterrents and treat for any other unwanted invaders.

Harvest. The last of your rhubarb – stop in mid July. Lots of crops including new potatoes and more soft fruits.

August

Sow. Spring cabbages, winter spinach, and more salads.

Jobs. Water everything during dry weather. Watch out for blight amongst your tomatoes and potatoes. If it appears cut it out at first sight.

Harvest. Your first batch of tomatoes, onions, sweet corn and anything else that looks ripe for the picking.

September

Jobs. Plant out autumn onion sets and Spring cabbages. Sort out strawberries by cutting away all leaves and getting rid of unwanted runners. When the raspberries have finished fruiting cut the canes right down to ground level.

Harvest. Everything that you can, including lots of tomatoes.

October

Sow. Broad beans for an early crop next year.

Jobs. Store all root vegetables.

Harvest. All your tomatoes even if they are green, as they will start to rot when it gets too cold. Make green tomato chutney.

November

Jobs. Clear all remains of crops and compost them. Store away hoses, pots and canes etc. Chop asparagus stems to ground level. Fork over all bare areas.

December

Jobs. Lift and divide rhubarb. Prune fruit bushes. Get your Christmas present list under control and add any new gardening items that you may need.

Basic Principles of Organic Gardening

Organic gardening is the science and art of growing fruit, vegetables and flowers successfully using natural processes, fertilisers and soil management.

Often with organic gardening the end result is not as pleasing to the eye, or as prolific as non-organic. But more often than not the taste and quality of vegetables using organic methods are better.

Managing soil is very important in an organic garden, adding lots of organic matter, (manure and compost) helps to keep it healthy and the healthier the plants the less likely they are to be attacked by insects.

Pest management is a big issue and imperative in any garden. Companion planting deters pests and attracts the right kind of insects, covering the plants with poly or net tunnels encourages more successful growth as well as preventing the pests from getting in. Crop rotation interrupts pest reproduction cycles. Keeping weeds down and a tidy garden leaves no hiding place for slugs.

Organic gardening is very easy for the everyday gardener and the only excuse for not doing it is if you don't know about it – But now you have read this you have no excuse. Hopefully you will have time to nurture your garden in the right way, it is well worth doing and it can be a lot cheaper than buying masses of chemicals.

Essential Gardening Equipment

Fork
Hoe
Watering can
Secateurs
Garden twine
Slug deterents
Bird netting or Haxnicks birdscare
Wheel barrow

Spade
Trowel
Good quality gloves
3 x poly tunnels
Bamboo canes for plant supports
Cloches (solar bells)
Rootrainers or seed trays for growing seeds in

I could get carried away but in order to keep it simple, I had better stop there as you can add all sorts of exciting things such as, plant bags, pots, fancy glass cloches...

Now all you need is a space to get started.

Asparagus

Sow Seeds in Greenhouse/on Windowsill: February
Sow Crowns Directly Outdoors: April to June
Transplant Outdoors: April to June
Depth to Plant: Seeds 1cm (1/2") – Crowns 10cm (5")
Distance Between Rows: 80cm (30")
Distance Between Plants: 50cm (20")
Harvest: May to 21st June (ish) – After you have waited at least two years for the plant to mature. If you pick it too soon you will ruin your crop for the future.

A Little Bit About The Crop

Asparagus starts off as a seed, but usually takes three to four years before you can feast from it, which is why a lot of seed sellers sell them as crowns – already established seeds. If you do grow asparagus from seed do not pick them until at least the third or even fourth year, when they will have strong roots. The French like to grow their asparagus under mounds blanching them, when the tops peek out they then cut them with a 25cm (10") cutter from 25cm (10") under the ground. This is what I would do here in the UK: Buy some already established crowns, plant them 10cm (5") deep in April and then wait until the following year for my first crop, which would be in May or June. When the asparagus has grown to roughly 15cm (6") get a sharp knife and cut it 5cm (2") under the ground. When the harvest is over let the asparagus grow into fun leafy plants and weed the area around them as they need whatever strength they can get. Asparagus are a perennial so can last for 20 years or so, if not dug up by accident.

Storage

Asparagus do not last for long, they are best eaten as fresh as possible. You can of course blanch them and then freeze them, but they are never as good.

Recipe

Clean and trim the asparagus, place in boiling water for 15 minutes, serve warm or cold with a hollandaise sauce. Scrumbalicious.

Aubergine

Sow Seeds in Greenhouse/on Windowsill: February to March
Sow Seeds Directly Outdoors: Wouldn't bother
Transplant Outdoors: May to June, only if you don't have a greenhouse
Depth to Plant: 1.5 cm (1/2")
Distance Between Rows: 30cm (12")
Distance Between Plants: 20cm (8")
Harvest: August to October – when roughly 10 - 18cm (4 - 7").

A Little Bit About The Crop

Ideally you need to sow aubergines early in seed trays, in a greenhouse. As the seedlings get larger you should then transplant them to single 7 - 10cm (3 - 4") pots, where they can grow on until the frosts have passed. In late May harden off the plants, add another dose of compost if you can before planting the seedlings out in your vegetable patch. Water as soon as you have planted. Aubergines like the warmth and not too much rain (although they do need to be watered if it is dry), so covering them with tunnels or cloches will help enormously.
As the aubergines grow they will become too heavy for the plant so tie them to a sturdy cane to take the weight, they are a similar crop to tomatoes so should be treated in the same way.

Storage

Not for long, best eaten fresh.

Recipe

Aubergine Crisps – a good canapé

1 Aubergine thinly sliced
Salt
Ground black pepper
100 ml Olive oil

Slice your aubergines, lay them onto either kitchen paper or a tea towel separately. Sprinkle salt over them liberally, this should encourage the water from the aubergines to come out and then be absorbed by the towels. After 10 minutes turn them over and repeat the process, then sprinkle a little pepper on. Heat up the olive oil in a pan, when it is boiling hot add the seasoned sliced aubergines, take them out when they are golden brown. Again place them onto a kitchen towel to absorb any extra fat. Eat them warm, beside a bowl of some sort of dip, like crème freche. Very Mediterranean.

Beans - climbing

Sow Seeds in Greenhouse/on Windowsill: March to July
Sow Seeds Directly Outdoors: May to July
Transplant Outdoors: May to August, when seedlings are between 15 - 30cm (6 - 12") high
Depth to Plant: 2.5cm (1")
Distance Between Rows: 45cm (18")
Distance Between Plants: 10 - 20cm (4 - 8")
Harvest: June - October

A Little Bit About The Crop

Beans are fairly easy to germinate. Sow the seeds into small pots or rootrainers, either in a greenhouse or on a windowsill. Water them well and leave them. It takes between 1 - 3 weeks for bean seeds to germinate. Do not let them dry out. When the seedlings have grown large enough plant them out in rows or in a circle if you are using a teepee cane support. To begin with cover them in cloches/tunnels to give them that extra boost, very soon (about 2 weeks later) you will need to support them. Make sure that the support you make is strong as when the wind blows - well you don't want your plants falling over now do you. When the beans are large enough, harvest them regularly as this will then stimulate the plant to produce more.

Storage

Blanche the beans and then freeze them. Or bottle them, putting as many as you can get into the jar.

Recipe
Monsieur Edouards Beans

Boil or steam 250 grammes (1/2 lb) beans until they are fairly soft (not crunchy). Fry in a pan on a medium heat, the beans, two chopped cloves of garlic, a knob of butter and a tablespoon of olive oil for 5 to 10 minutes. Add salt to taste. The beans go very well beside a stew or a roast.

Beans - dwarf

Sow Seeds in Greenhouse/on Windowsill: March to July
Sow Seeds Directly Outdoors: May to July (If you must)
Transplant Outdoors: May to August, when the seedlings are between 15 - 30cm (6 - 12") high
Depth to Plant: 2.5cm (1")
Distance Between Rows: 45cm (18")
Distance Between Plants: 30cm (12")
Harvest: June to October

A Little Bit About The Crop
Beans are fairly easy to germinate. Sow the seeds into small pots or rootrainers, either in a greenhouse or on a windowsill. Water them well and leave them. It takes between 1 - 3 weeks for bean seeds to germinate. Do not let them dry out. When the seedlings have grown large enough plant them out in rows. To begin with cover them in cloches/tunnels to give them that extra boost. The beans will grow into little bushes. When the beans are large enough, harvest them regularly as this will then stimulate the plant to grow more.

Storage
Blanche the beans and then freeze them. Or Bottle them, putting as many as you can get into the jar.

Point
Children love growing beans as they grow so quickly, they can also reach the dwarf variety.

Beetroot

Sow Seeds in Greenhouse/on Windowsill: March to May
Sow Seeds Directly Outdoors: April to July
Transplant Outdoors: April to June, when large enough to handle, about 6 weeks after sowing
Depth to Plant: 1.5cm (1/2")
Distance Between Rows: 30cm (12")
Distance Between Plants: 5 - 7cm (2 - 3")
Harvest: Salad leaves in June and July, golf ball sized beets in July and August and the main crop from July to October.

A Little Bit About The Crop
You can either sow seeds in 7 - 10cm (3 - 4") pots, 3 seeds per pot. Or you can happily sow them directly into the vegetable patch, but if you sow them directly you must wait a little for the weather to warm up slightly. When the seedlings are large enough to handle, plant them out carefully, at this stage they can be 2 - 5cm (1 - 2") apart. Using a poly tunnel encourages earlier growth and better results – don't forget to water them. As they grow you may want to harvest some of the young tender leaves for your salads, and then pull up every other beet to eat when they are golf ball size. This will leave enough space for your main crop to grow to its maximum size. By the Autumn the beets will be at their full size, hopefully something like a snooker ball.

Storage
1. Leave in the ground until you need them.
2. Dry store – cleaning gently, place carefully in a box of sand in a cool room that is frost free.
3. Pickling.
4. Freezing.

Tip
When buying seeds, try to buy ones that are resistant to bolting 'Bolthardy' is a good variety. Barabietola di Chioggia is a pretty variety with pink and white circles within.

Broad beans

Sow Seeds in Greenhouse/on Windowsill: October to November or January
Sow Seeds Directly Outdoors: October to November or January to February
Transplant Outdoors: When they are large enough to handle
Depth to Plant: 5 - 7cm (2 - 3")
Distance Between Rows: 30cm (12")
Distance Between Plants: 22cm (9"). Sow in double rows, this means sow two rows 20cm (9") apart, and all the plants 20cm (9") apart.
Harvest: April - September

A Little Bit About The Crop
I usually sow my seeds on the windowsill or in the greenhouse in January, in a rootrainer or in small pots. When the seeds have grown to an easy to handle size, plant out in double rows. The beans may need support from small canes if they are in a windy position. When the plants flower and are beginning to show the pods, pinch off a couple of inches from the top of the plant. This will direct the energy towards the pods rather than into new growth. This also reduces the aphids invasion. Before harvesting, make sure that the beans within the pods are large enough. They should be about 1/3 of the weight of the pod.

Storage
1. To freeze them, first you blanch them, let them cool, and then bag them.
2. Dry them out and keep them in an airtight container.

Point
Broad beans in flower have a wonderful smell.

Broccoli - purple sprouting

Sow Seeds in Greenhouse/on Windowsill: March to April
Sow Seeds Directly Outdoors: April to May
Transplant Outdoors: May to July
Depth to Plant: 2cm (3/4")
Distance Between Rows: 45cm (18")
Distance Between Plants: 30cm (12")
Harvest: December to April

A Little Bit About The Crop

Purple sprouting broccoli is the hardiest and easiest broccoli to grow, it is high in antioxidants which are good for you.

I like to grow my seeds in either small 8cm (3") pots or in rapid rootrainers. Alternatively sow them thinly, directly into their rows, remembering to thin them out when the seedlings are between 8 - 15cm (3"- 6") tall to 30cm (12") apart. Keep well watered during dry periods and watch out for slugs when the plants are small. Also keep a careful eye on any caterpillars that appear, picking them off and squishing them or cover with mesh to keep them out. As winter comes earth up around the stems of the plants to keep them from falling over in the wind. You may find that you need to put stakes next to them for extra support. Harvest them from December onwards, cutting off the central 'sprout' first when it is between 10 - 15cm (4" - 6"). Harvest regularly as the more you pick them the more they grow. When the broccoli flowers, that is the end of your broccoli as it becomes tasteless and chewy.

Storage

Either blanch the broccoli for 3 minutes and then freeze it, or keep it in a cool place for anything up to 4 days.

Tip

Eat as soon as you can after harvesting.
Great healthy winter vegetable when not a lot else is growing.
Tastes similar to asparagus.

Brussels Sprouts

Sow Seeds in Greenhouse/on Windowsill: March to April
Sow Seeds Directly Outdoors: April
Transplant Outdoors: May to June
Depth to Plant: 2cm (1")
Distance Between Rows: 75cm (30")
Distance Between Plants: 75cm (30")
Harvest: September to February

A Little Bit About The Crop

Sow the seeds into small pots or rootrainers in the greenhouse or on a windowsill. Plant out when they are between 10 - 15cm (4 - 6") tall. If you are sowing them outside, sow them very thinly. As the seeds come up thin them out even more, by either transplanting them or getting rid of the smaller weaker ones. Finally plant them out in their final positions, 75cm (30") apart. Keep them under poly tunnels or netting for as long as you can, in order to keep them safe from birds and pests. Watch out for the caterpillars, aphids and slugs, there are concoctions that you can buy or make, or you can squish them off. As Autumn comes build up the earth around the base of the stems, this should hold them firm, some Brussels sprouts could do with a cane to support them especially in windy areas.

Harvest the sprouts from the bottom up, taking only a few from each plant. If any plants have 'blown' get rid of them as they will be using up valuable energy that could be going into the other sprouts.

Storage

Not for long, about two weeks in a cool place.

Recipe

When preparing to cook, place a cross with your knife 1/2 cm (1/4") deep on the bottom of the sprout. This enables equal cooking throughout.

Cabbage

Sow Seeds in Greenhouse/on Windowsill: February to April, summer/autumn crop
April to May, winter crop
July to August, spring crop
Sow Seeds Directly Outdoors: From February onwards
Transplant Outdoors: When the seedlings are about 8 - 9cm (3") tall
Depth to Plant: 2cm (3/4")
Distance Between Rows: 30cm (12")
Distance Between Plants: 30cm (12")
Harvest: All year.

A Little Bit About The Crop

There are many different varieties of cabbage depending on when you want the crop. Cabbages are something that you can harvest all year round – although you may just get bored of them! Sow the seeds in small pots or rootrainers, when they are about 9cm (3") tall plant them out in their final positions. Make sure that you stamp down well but carefully the soil around, as cabbages like firm ground not fluffy. Now this crop tends to take up quite a lot of space as with the brussels sprouts, so decide carefully about how many you actually want. Be very wary of slugs and snails, of birds and caterpillars. I personally use either a net tunnel or poly tunnel for the birds and whenever I see caterpillars, usually on the underside of the leaf, I squish them between my fingers or stamp on them. When harvesting cut off the cabbage head close to the ground. Cut a 1cm (1/2") deep cross into the stump, this should encourage another smaller crop of cabbages.

Storage

Remove the roots and outer leaves, place in a straw lined box in a cool dry area. They can last for at least three or four months.

Recipe

Slice the cabbage up, place in a pan with 1cm (1/2") of cold water add a decent sized knob of butter, a clove of chopped garlic and a little salt. Put over a medium heat, let it simmer until virtually all the water has gone – about 5 - 10 minutes. This is a way of cooking cabbages to go with anything, it brings out the sweetness and is very moorish, even my children love it.

Carrots

Sow Seeds in Greenhouse/on Windowsill: Not really
Sow Seeds Directly Outdoors: March to April, summer crop
                                  April to July, main winter crop
Transplant Outdoors: No
Depth to Plant: 2cm (3/4")
Distance Between Rows: 15cm (6")
Distance Between Plants: 5cm (2")
Harvest: June to July, summer crop and September to October, main winter crop.

A Little Bit About The Crop

Don't add manure here! Carrots are not too fussy about their soils but the sandier and lighter the better. Make sure that the soil has been well tilled and then dig out your rows, 2cm (3/4") deep. Very thinly sow your seeds. More often than not the carrots will be overcrowded and you will need to thin them out. This means being very brutal and pulling up the smaller plants leaving spaces of 5cm (2") between each plant, this gives the carrots space to grow to a proper size. When you pull up the unwanted plants do it gently so as not to let off too many smells of the bruised foliage, as this will attract the carrot fly - something you don't want to do. Harvest the carrots from June onwards. Summer carrots are usually sweeter and smaller, winter carrots are more for the casserole pot, but home grown carrots are doubly more delicious than bought ones.

Storage

Use the winter crop carrots for storage. Cut off the leaves 1 cm (1/4") from the top of the carrot, place the carrots in layers of sand or peat in a cool dry shed. Do not let the carrots touch otherwise they will infect each other if they go bad. Carrots can last until March in this way.

Tip

The fight against carrot fly!
To avoid pests such as carrot fly, try companion planting with onions or use a fleece or micromesh tunnel to keep them out.

Cauliflowers

Sow Seeds in Greenhouse/on Windowsill: January to March, summer crop
April to July, winter crop

Sow Seeds Directly Outdoors: A bit dodgy

Transplant Outdoors: March to May, summer crop
July to October, winter crop

Depth to Plant: 2cm (3/4")

Distance Between Rows: Summer crop 45cm (18"), Winter crop 60cm (24")

Distance Between Plants: Same as above

Harvest: All year round if you do both! June to October, summer crop
November to May, winter crop

A Little Bit About The Crop

I would recommend starting the seeds off in a greenhouse or on the windowsill, in pots or root trainers. When the seedlings are large enough to handle plant them out into their final positions. The soil needs to be firm, not light and fluffy. If you have a poly or net tunnel put this over them as it adds protection from pests and weather. Be careful of slugs, they love young plants. Summer cauliflowers require more attention than winter ones as they need watering during dry periods and it is harder to get the perfect cauliflower. Depending on how many cauliflowers you have, you may like to pick some when they are small so that you don't have too many all at once. If you wait too long to harvest them, they will bolt, so watch out. Cut the cauliflowers either in the morning or evening, or in the case of frost, cut at midday.

Storage

You can freeze them, by cutting the cauliflower up into florets, blanching them with a little lemon juice and putting them in the freezer. You can pull up the entire plant and hang it upside down in a cool place, it should last for three to four weeks like this.

Tip

Bend external leaves over the cauliflower to protect it from the weather and pests.

Celery

Sow Seeds in Greenhouse/on Windowsill: February to March
Sow Seeds Directly Outdoors: Not really
Transplant Outdoors: May to June
Depth to Plant: 1/2cm (1/2")
Distance Between Rows: 22cm (9")
Distance Between Plants: 22cm (9")
Harvest: August to October

A Little Bit About The Crop

I sow my seeds in seed trays in a greenhouse or on a windowsill in February, then when they are large enough to transplant I put them into small 7.5cm (3") pots. When they have 5 or 6 leaves on, harden them off and then plant them in their final positions. They should be fairly close to each other as they provide each other with shade, so perhaps plant a square for them rather than a row. If there is still a fear of frost, plant them under poly tunnels or cloches. When harvesting, dig them up with a trowel so as not to disturb their neighbours.

There are two types of celery – self blanching and not self blanching. For the traditional 'not self blanching' variety you need to plant them in trenches and when they get to about 30cm (1ft) high you then pile up the earth around the stalks. As the celery grows, keep placing earth up the sides, by the end of September only the top leaves should be showing. If there is a frost they will die, unless covered up. Now all this sounds incredibly complicated, so there are seeds that you can buy that are self blanching - way easier. Just plant the plants out normally in May or June and harvest them from August until the first frosts.

Storage Store in cool place for three to five days.

Point

Herbalists recommend celery for reducing blood pressure.

Chilli Peppers

Sow Seeds in Greenhouse/on Windowsill: February to April
Sow Seeds Directly Outdoors: Not recommended in England
Transplant Outdoors: June, or better still keep them in the greenhouse
Depth to Plant: Seeds 1cm (1/2")
Distance Between Rows: 30cm - 45cm (12" - 18")
Distance Between Plants: 30cm - 45cm (12" - 18")
Harvest: August to October

A Little Bit About The Crop

These are very much a greenhouse or sunny windowsill pot vegetable. Sow the seeds into seed trays and when they are large enough to handle pot them on into 7.5cm (3") pots. Now when the chillies grow out of these, either transplant them into the vegetable patch or into larger pots, about 20cm (8") wide. They will need a small cane to hold the plants up like tomatoes. If planting outside, keep them covered with a cloche or poly tunnel for as long as possible, somewhere in the sun. Chillies in pots should have their tops pinched off to make them sturdier, bushier and stronger. Like their cousins capsicums, chillies come in various colours, lengths and strengths.

Storage

I recommend placing the whole chilli into the lowest heat oven overnight to dry out, then you can keep them for between 3 - 6 months.

Tip

Don't pick your nose after chopping chillies, it will sting like mad.

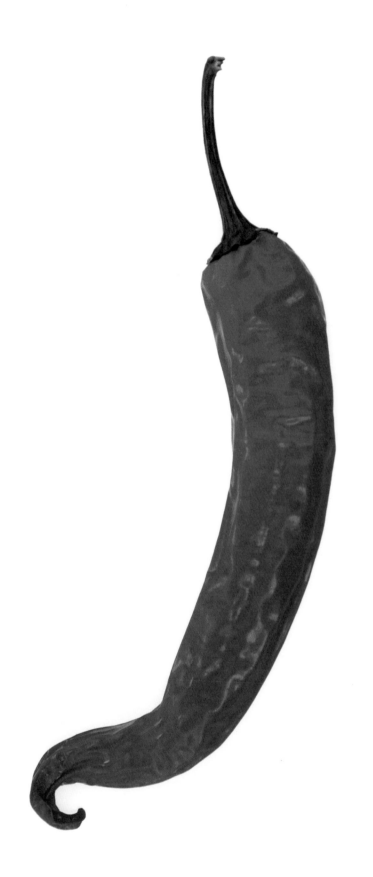

Courgettes & Squashes

Sow Seeds in Greenhouse/on Windowsill: April to June
Sow Seeds Directly Outdoors: May
Transplant Outdoors: May to July
Depth to Plant: 1cm (1/2")
Distance Between Rows: 60cm (24")
Distance Between Plants: 60cm (24")
Harvest: July to October

A Little Bit About The Crop

One of the easiest vegetables to grow once germinated and incredibly satisfying. I usually
soak mine overnight in water then sow them in small pots 7.5cm (3") on the windowsill or in the
greenhouse. You can do this outside but there is a danger of slugs polishing them off. From May
onwards harden off the plants, when they are as large as you dare let them grow in the small pots,
plant them in their final positions. Courgettes love a good dollop of manure under them, so if you
have any dig it into the ground before you plant them. They do need quite a lot of space as they
grow pretty large. I like to grow a variety of different courgettes and squash, say 2 plants of each
variety. There are seed companies that sell a variety pack. Pick the courgettes anything from 15cm
(6") to 30cm (12"), depending on what you want to do with them. The smaller they are the more
tender and more delicious. The larger are good for perhaps stuffed courgette dishes. The flower is
also edible either fried or in a salad.

Storage

Courgettes last for about 2 weeks kept in a cool place to keep the skins soft, but the fresher you
eat them the better they are. Later in the season they grow very big very quickly, I put the larger
marrows and squashes on the path to harden for two days and then keep them in the garden shed
until March.

Recipe

A lot of children don't like courgettes. I get mine to eat them like this.
Slice up 3 medium sized courgettes 20cm (8") into 'coin' shapes, place them in a pan with 2cm (1")
of water and a pinch of salt. Boil them slowly for about 5 minutes until tender. When they are
cooked, put them in the liquidiser with a large knob of butter and two tablespoons of crème freche.
Whizz them up and serve them as a vegetable puree.

Point

Did you know that you can either fry the courgette flowers in batter or eat them in a salad.

Cucumbers

Sow Seeds in Greenhouse/on Windowsill: March to May
Sow Seeds Directly Outdoors: May
Transplant Outdoors: May to June
Depth to Plant: 1cm (1/2")
Distance Between Rows: 45cm (18")
Distance Between Plants: 45cm (18")
Harvest: July to October

A Little Bit About The Crop

I normally sow my seeds into 7.5cm (3") pots in late March and then put them on a windowsill or in the greenhouse. When they are large enough re pot them as they will outgrow their little pots before it is time to plant them out. In May harden off the plants for a few days and then transplant them to their final positions about 45cm (18") apart. Keep them under a cloche or poly tunnel to give them that extra boost and to keep any birds or pests off. Watch out for slugs! Cucumbers tend to climb and creep about, so pinch out the growing tips to keep the energies focused on producing quality cucumbers. Cucumbers like to be kept moist so need plenty of water. There are two types of cucumbers - the all female variety (modern): This is an easier variety where you don't have to pick the male flowers. You get more fruit but they are shorter. The ordinary variety (traditional): With this type you have to look at the flowers, leave the ones with cucumbers growing behind them and pick the ones with nothing behind them. If you don't pick the male flowers they pollinate the female ones and make the cucumbers taste bitter.

Storage

If kept in a cool place they will last for about 2 - 3 weeks.

Tip

Grow your cucumbers in a greenhouse if possible. Cucumbers are 96% water – so water them well!

Endive / Chicory

Sow Seeds in Greenhouse/on Windowsill: April to May
Sow Seeds Directly Outdoors: May to August
Transplant Outdoors: May
Depth to Plant: 1cm (1/2")
Distance Between Rows: 30cm (12")
Distance Between Plants: 30cm (12")
Harvest: August to March

A Little Bit About The Crop

A good Winter salad! Endives are a continental type of lettuce, they can be bitter unless you blanch them by covering with a blacked out pot during their last few weeks of growth, this makes them sweeter. Endives are a bit of an acquired taste. Sow very thinly either outside directly or into rootrainers or 6 - 8cm (3 - 4") pots. When the plants are large enough, thin them out leaving only the best. Re plant them into their final positions 25cm (10") apart. As they grow they will look a little like a green mop head. When they are almost large enough to eat cover them with a pot, covering any holes so as not to let any light in. By mid August they should be ready for harvesting. Endive is great as a cut and come again vegetable, so cut them about 2cm (1") from the ground. Watch out for greedy snails and don't forget to water when the ground is dry.

Storage

Only for about one week in a cool place.

Recipe
Chicory and Tomato Salad – that looks fun and is very easy

1 chicory for 3 people
About 15 baby tomatoes
Feta cheese
Mayonnaise
White wine vinegar, salt and pepper

Save the large outer leaves of the chicory as bowls to put your chopped chicory, tomatoes and feta into. Place all the ingredients into the leaves on separate plates. Mix a little white wine vinegar with the mayonnaise to make it more runny, add salt and pepper to taste. Pour the mayonnaise either onto or around your chicory bowls.

Fennel

Sow Seeds in Greenhouse/on Windowsill: February to March
Sow Seeds Directly Outdoors: April to May
Transplant Outdoors: April to May
Depth to Plant: 1cm (1/2")
Distance Between Rows: 25cm (10")
Distance Between Plants: 25cm (10")
Harvest: July to November

A Little Bit About The Crop

Fennel can be eaten in a crunchy salad or roasted as a vegetable that goes well with fish or chicken. It has a wonderful aniseed taste (you either like it or you don't). Of course it is also a rather impressive and beautiful vegetable to grow. Either sow the seeds directly into drills in your vegetable patch about 1cm (1/2") deep, or sow into 6 - 8cm (3 - 4") pots or rootrainers. As the seedlings appear, thin them out so that only the best are left in the pots and in your rows outside. Plants should be 25cm (10") apart, when in their final positions. Use a cloche or poly tunnel to protect them from weather and pests during their first few weeks. Harvest the fennel from late July onwards, cut the bulbs 2.5cm (1") from the earth as they may grow again.

Storage

Keep in a cool place for up to three weeks.

Point

Fennel is rarely troubled by pests and will do well in almost any kind of soil.

Garlic

Sow Seeds in Greenhouse/on Windowsill: Not really
Sow Seeds Directly Outdoors: October to November and February to March
Depth to Plant: Just below the soil surface
Distance Between Rows: 20cm (8")
Distance Between Plants: 10cm (4")
Harvest: May to September

A Little Bit About The Crop

There is nothing more mouth watering than the smell of garlic being fried. The reason to grow your own garlic would be to ward off unwanted pests in your vegetable patch as well as to eat your own home grown variety. Sow the garlic in individual cloves about 10cm (4") apart. If you sow them in the autumn you will get a larger crop than if you sow in the Spring. Garlic loves to flower, cut off the stem before it does and this will concentrate the plant's energy on the crop beneath. Harvest the garlic from June onwards by pulling it out of the ground as you would a weed. Leave it to dry in the sun for a few days before storing.

Storage

Stored in a cool dry place garlic can last between 4 - 6 months.

Point

Garlic is unbelievably good for you, it can lower blood pressure, fat and cholesterol levels. It combats bacterial, fungal and viral infections.

Kale

Sow Seeds in Greenhouse/on Windowsill: March to April
Sow Seeds Directly Outdoors: April to August
Transplant Outdoors: May to September
Depth to Plant: 1cm (1/2")
Distance Between Rows: 60cm (24")
Distance Between Plants: 60cm (24")
Harvest: November to April

A Little Bit About The Crop

Kale is another brassica crop, cooked in the right way it is delicious or you can eat the small leaves in a salad. In times gone by it was used to feed the cattle during the winter as it is full of nutrients. I would sow mine in the greenhouse or on a windowsill in 6 - 10cm (3 - 4") pots. When the seedlings appear prick out the baddies leaving only 1 strong plant per pot. Transplant the seedlings to their final positions from May onwards when they are about 6 - 15cm (3 - 6") tall, put cloches or a poly tunnel over them to protect them from weather and pests. For fully grown Kale, plant out 60cm (24") apart, but for the more tender smaller leaves plant out at 30cm (12"). Watch out for slugs when the plants are small and of course for the caterpillars and aphids. If you find that there are too many to pinch off you may have to resort to some kind of crop saver spray. Harvest the crop from November to April cutting the leaves off as you need them, sometimes they can grow again after they have been cut.

Storage

Store in a cool place and they will last for about 10 days. Or blanch, cut up, place in a freezer bag and then put in the deep freezer.

Tip

Plant nasturtiums nearby as they attract white butterflies and keep them off your Kale and other brassicas.

Leeks

Sow Seeds in Greenhouse/on Windowsill: February to April
Sow Seeds Directly Outdoors: March to April
Transplant Outdoors: May to July
Depth to Plant: 2cm (3/4")
Distance Between Rows: 30cm (12")
Distance Between Plants: 15cm (6")
Harvest: September to May

A Little Bit About The Crop

There are three main varieties – early, mid season and late. So decide which ones you want to have or get all three. I would just go for one variety as I like as many different vegetables growing in my patch and only have room for one variety. Sow your seeds into rootrainers or small 8cm (3") pots. Thin them out to one per section or pot. In June or July when the leeks are about 20cm (8") tall, plant them into their final positions. Water them well. Harvest your leeks either as pencil thin baby leeks or as fully grown 8cm (3") diameter ones. When the flower begins to grow on top the leek turns into a woody stem and is too tough to eat. But the flower will then produce seeds that you can happily collect to use the following year, or you can use them in a stunning flower arrangement.

Storage

Leeks last in the ground for most of the winter or store them in a cool place for 1 to 2 weeks.

Recipe
Chicken and Leek Pie

3 chicken breasts diced	1 clove of garlic chopped.
3 medium leeks chopped	Olive oil for frying.
Salt and pepper to taste	200 ml crème freche.
Mashed potatoes	Cheddar cheese grated for topping (optional)

Fry the chicken and garlic until brown. Place in oven proof dish. Fry leeks until brown, place in dish. Add salt, pepper and crème freche, mix all the ingredients together. Place the mashed potato on top and pop into the oven for 30 minutes at a medium temperature. If you like, add grated cheese on the top five minutes before taking out of the oven. This goes well with a salad.

Lettuces

Sow Seeds in Greenhouse/on Windowsill: January to September
Sow Seeds Directly Outdoors: April to September
Transplant Outdoors: April to October
Depth to Plant: 2cm (3/4")
Distance Between Rows: 30cm (12")
Distance Between Plants: 30cm (12") depending on the type
Harvest: All year round

A Little Bit About The Crop

The key to eating and harvesting lettuces to have all summer long, is to plant them out at regular intervals, otherwise they will all be ready to harvest at the same time. I would also plant out a variety of lettuces – using small amounts from each packet of seeds. So decide which lettuces you want and when you want them. Lettuces are versatile and can grow in between plants. Sow the seeds on a windowsill or in the greenhouse from January onwards, depending on their variety and when you want them. Sow them into root trainers or small 8cm (3") pots. When they are large enough to handle plant them out into their final positions. Beware of slugs and birds. I would use a cloche or poly tunnels for protection while they are small. When harvesting either cut the entire lettuce off the root using a knife, this may well sprout another lettuce again. Or you can pick the leaves gently off as you need them, they should grow more.

Storage

Just a few days in a cool place.

Tip

Grow several varieties at the same time to get a good colourful tasty mix of salad leaves.
Don't let your lettuces lie in the sun after picking them, while you are busy doing other things in the garden – they will wilt. Try a cut and come again variety as they are less work and take up less space.

Melon

Sow Seeds in Greenhouse/on Windowsill: March to May
Sow Seeds Directly Outdoors: Not a good idea
Transplant Outdoors: June to July
Depth to Plant: 2cm (3/4")
Distance Between Rows: 50cm (20")
Distance Between Plants: 50cm (20")
Harvest: August to September

A Little Bit About The Crop

Melons like the warmth of a greenhouse for as long as possible, then when you plant them out they should be covered with a cloche or a poly tunnel. Sow your seeds as early as you can, preferably on a windowsill where there is warmth, one seed per 8cm (3") pot. Let the plant grow as large as your hand and then plant it out in a well manured position. Watch out for the slugs at this stage, they love young tender plants. Melons like to crawl along the ground getting muddled up between your other vegetables, just let them. The manure will make a huge difference on their size and quality. Make sure that the melons have priority in the patch for as much sunlight as possible, otherwise they will never ripen and be a waste of space. Preferably, if you have the kind of greenhouse where you can grow melons, they would rather be in the greenhouse, and well watered. Harvest the melons when they are large enough and start to ripen, you can tell they are ripe when they smell sweet.

Storage

For up to two weeks in a cool dry place.

Recipe

A simple but delicious French starter is a slice of melon served with a piece of Parma ham draped over the top and a vinaigrette. Add either a sprig of parsley or basil for decoration. The sweetness of the melon brings out the flavour of the Parma ham.

Mushrooms

Sow Grain Spawn in Greenhouse, Shed, Cold Frame or Cellar: All year round but temperature
must be between 10° and 18°C

Sow Seeds Directly Outdoors: N/A
Transplant Outdoors: N/A
Depth to Plant: N/A
Distance Between Rows: N/A
Distance Between Plants: N/A
Harvest: 5 - 25 weeks after planting, depending on the type.

A Little Bit About The Crop

Wow – mushrooms. They are not the ordinary easy crop that every gardener grows by any means.
There are different varieties and different ways of buying the spawn. In plugs – to hammer directly
onto a piece of wood. Grain - that you sprinkle onto manure. Blocks - that you plant and various
kits. I think that the best way to start is with a kit, which comes with the compost or straw, but you
must follow the instructions well. If you are feeling a little more daring and have access to compost
or stable manure, you can grow your own in buckets or tubs, in the shade, a greenhouse, shed,
cellar or covered cold frame (depending on temperature). The compost must remain moist, not wet
or dry. When harvesting the mushrooms, harvest gently so as not to disturb the remaining spawn.
You can of course grow mushrooms in the corner of your garden using 'blocks' of spawn. Plant
them 6cm (2") deep and 30cm (12") apart. Again this is risky and you can't mow the lawn. The
natural alternative is to go for an autumn walk in the woods and gather wild mushrooms. But
beware! Make sure they are not poisonous.

Storage

Best kept in a cool place for about 1 week - maximum.

Recipe
War Time Mushrooms on Toast

Cut up 1 clove of garlic and add it to a frying pan of melted butter. Cut up a large handful
of mushrooms and add to the pan. Fry until brown, tip onto a piece of toast and eat hot.

Onions - seeds

Sow Seeds in Greenhouse/on Windowsill: February to April
Sow Seeds Directly Outdoors: No - as it is easier to sow them and then transplant into their right positions
Transplant Outdoors: May to June
Depth to Plant: 1cm (1/2")
Distance Between Rows: 22cm (9")
Distance Between Plants: 4 - 10cm (1 1/2" - 4") for smaller onions
15 - 25cm (6" - 10") for larger onions
Harvest: July to October

A Little Bit About The Crop

The advantage of growing onions from seeds and not sets is that it is far cheaper especially if you are going for a big harvest. Sow the seeds on a windowsill or in the greenhouse, then transplant them when they are about 8cm (3"). Plant them vertically into the ground, being gentle. The bulb should be 1cm (1/2") below the surface. Depending on the onion's final sizes, plant them between 4 - 25cm (2 - 10") apart. It is important to keep the weeds down as this can affect the size of your onions. Water when dry. When the leaves start to turn yellow at the ends, bend the tops over to help with the ripening, possibly even clear a little of the soil at the top of the bulb. Lift the onions as you need them, but don't let them rot in the ground, so harvest and store them before the end of October. After you lift them let them lie in the sun for a couple of days.

Storage

Only store the onions that are perfect. Store them either in jute storage bags hung up or in old tights knotting after each onion. They can keep in a well aired room for up to six months.

Recipe
Red Onion Marmalade - to make 5 jars

2 kg Red onions, finely sliced
280 gms brown sugar
200 ml of any kind of vinegar
100 ml of balsamic vinegar

Slowly fry the onions for about 40 minutes. Add sugar, mixing occasionally on a low heat until sugar has dissolved. Add the vinegar and one teaspoon of salt. Boil it up until thick and gooey. Take off the heat and put into jars straight away.

Onions - sets

Sow Sets in Greenhouse/on Windowsill: No
Sow Sets Directly Outdoors: March to April or September to October
Transplant Outdoors: No
Depth to Plant: So that the pointy tips are just below the surface of the soil
Distance Between Rows: 22cm (9")
Distance Between Plants: 4 - 10cm (1 1/2" - 4") for smaller onions
                                          15 - 25cm (6" - 10") for larger onions
Harvest: May to October

A Little Bit About The Crop
Make sure that your soil is well rotavated and fertilised, onions like a well drained and sunny area – so do most plants! There are many different varieties of onions, so choose something that you would like, maybe something out of the ordinary like giant onions that you can show off or red onions. Depending on the onions (final) size, plant them between 4 - 25cm (2 - 10") apart. It is important to keep the weeds down as this can affect the size of your onions. Water when dry. When the leaves start to turn yellow at the ends, bend the tops over to help with the ripening, possibly even clear a little of the soil at the top of the bulb. Lift the onions as you need them, but don't let them rot in the ground, so harvest and store them before the end of October. After you lift them let them lie in the sun for a couple of days.

Storage
Only store the onions that are perfect. Store them either in jute storage bags hung up or in old tights knotting after each onion. They can keep in a well aired room for up to six months.

Tip
When peeling and chopping onions, light a couple of candles, this should stop your eyes watering, as the vapours from the onions will be absorbed in the candle flames.
Always fry onions slowly.

Parsnips

Sow Seeds in Greenhouse/on Windowsill: No
Sow Seeds Directly Outdoors: March to May
Transplant Outdoors: No
Depth to Plant: 2cm (3/4")
Distance Between Rows: 30cm (12")
Distance Between Plants: 15cm (6")
Harvest: August to March

A Little Bit About The Crop

Parsnips are not to everyone's taste. The seeds take a long time to germinate and the plants take a long time to grow and they hog a space in the patch. But they are a winter vegetable and need little attention. You can plant various quick growing things like radishes or lettuces during the summer months in between them to conserve space. Sow the seeds in their final positions from March onwards, germination can take around one month. Cover the seeds with a cloche or poly tunnel to protect them from birds and pests, also to give them a bit more warmth to encourage germination. Thin out if necessary, as they should be 15cm (6") apart. Normally the first harvest of parsnips is after the first frost, but you can pick them before if you would like some tender baby ones. It all depends how you like them.

Storage

Parsnips keep well in the ground until about mid February. In February lift any remaining parsnips and store them in a jute bag, or even better a box of sand (bit of a hassle), not touching each other in a cool dark place.

Recipe
Roast Parsnips

Peel and cut the parsnips in two lengthways. Place in an oven proof dish – cover with olive oil and honey. Sprinkle a little cumin and salt over the top and then roast in a medium oven for about one hour, until the parsnips are golden brown and soft in the middle.

Peas & Mange tout

Sow Seeds in Greenhouse/on Windowsill: February to March
Sow Seeds Directly Outdoors: October to November or March to June
Transplant Outdoors: May to June
Depth to Plant: 4cm (2")
Distance Between Rows: 75cm (30")
Distance Between Plants: 10cm (4")
Harvest: May to October

A Little Bit About The Crop
The fresher you eat the peas the sweeter they be. My children love just picking them straight from the garden and eating them, in fact when I garden with the children it is a crop that they usually choose to grow. As soon as you pick the peas the sugar turns to starch, so the less time between the picking and the placing on the table the better. Mangetout may be a better choice as you eat the entire pod, rather than just the peas, the choice is yours. Sow the seeds either in small pots or even better in root trainers as this helps the roots not to get mixed up and then torn when transplanting. Sow them 4 cm (2") deep and don't let the seeds dry out. When they are about 15cm (6") high, transplant them outdoors, I have great fun making wigwam shapes with canes for support or you can of course plant out in rows, making a lengthy tent shape with the canes. To help the peas to grip the canes tie them with a little soft tie or garden twine. Watch out for the slugs, snails, mice and birds, put down slug deterrents, and cover them with either netting or some kind of cloche. Keep moist.

Storage
Freeze when fresh, otherwise they can be kept in the fridge for about three days.

Tip
Enjoy your peas fresh, don't expect to grow mountains, and watch out for the thieving birds.

Peppers

Sow Seeds in Greenhouse/on Windowsill: February to March
Sow Seeds Directly Outdoors: Probably won't work
Transplant Outdoors: May to June
Depth to Plant: 1cm (1/2")
Distance Between Rows: 45cm (18")
Distance Between Plants: 45cm (18")
Harvest: August to November

A Little Bit About The Crop

This is a crop that when grown in England is much better off in the greenhouse or on a windowsill in pots for as long as possible. If it is to be planted outside I would plant it in a sunny but sheltered spot keeping a cloche on top, bearing in mind that the flowers have to be pollinated at some point. Sow the seeds in a tray. The seeds take between 2 - 4 weeks to germinate, when the seedlings are large enough, pot them into 9cm (3") pots. Get rid of the weaker plants, keep only the best. In June either transfer them to their final position in the vegetable patch or into bigger 20 - 30cm (8 - 12") pots and keep them in the greenhouse. Place a sturdy cane beside them and as with tomatoes tie them onto the cane. For the pots, pinch out the tops of the plants to make them bushier.
You get all sorts of types of peppers, when choosing I would go for a hardy and early variety. Peppers also vary in colours, mostly they go from green to red, but you can get yellow ones and even purplish brown ones.

Storage

If you keep them cool they can last for up to 3 weeks.

Recipe

Place the whole pepper onto an oven proof dish, cook for 10 minutes in a hot oven, until the 1st layer of skin is burnt looking. Take it out of the oven, wrap in newspaper and leave it to steam for another 5 minutes in its parcel. Unwrap it, then peel the outer layer of skin off, take out the pips, and slice into strips of about 1cm (1/2")thick. Put onto a plate add a tiny bit of chopped garlic, olive oil and salt and pepper. Delicious served on a hot Summers day, with other salads.

Potatoes

Sow Seeds in Greenhouse/on Windowsill: No
Sow Seeds Directly Outdoors: February to April
Transplant Outdoors: No
Depth to Plant: 10cm (4") for earlies, 20cm (8") for main crop
Distance Between Rows: 60cm (24") for earlies, 75cm (30") for main crop
Distance Between Plants: 30cm (12") for earlies, 38cm (15") for main crop
Harvest: May to October

A Little Bit About The Crop

Potatoes can be so cheap to buy from the shops that you are not likely to be growing your own to save money, so why not when you are choosing which ones to grow, go for flavour. As soon as you buy your seed potatoes lay them out on a tray or in open egg boxes in a cool but frost free place; light but not in the sun for about 6 weeks. This will help them to produce chits (sprouty root things). Make sure that before you plant, the potato bed has been turned over well. You can warm up the beds by placing mini poly tunnels over them a few days before planting. Plant the potato seeds (tubers) between 10cm (4") (earlies) and 20cm (8") (main crop) deep. Place a poly tunnel over them to keep the soil warm. As the shoots begin to appear earth up around them making small mounds. Keep the poly tunnels on them to protect them from late frosts. Early potatoes take between 12 - 15 weeks to mature, main crop take about 20 weeks. Blight is an infection that rots the leaves, roots and eventually the new potatoes, it normally comes with wet warm weather in late summer. If you spot it on the leaves, chop off the leaves as soon as you can and hope for the best. Alternatively you can spray them against blight in June.

If you find that you have no space for growing potatoes, why not grow them in a potato bag. Directions: Add 10cm (4") of compost into the bottom of the bag. Place 5 tubers evenly in the bag. Cover with 5cm (2") of more compost. As the potato plants grow add more and more compost leaving just the tips of the leaves each time. When the compost reaches the top of the bag let them grow until two weeks after they have flowered when you can harvest them.

Storage

Dig the potatoes up by the end of October and store the good ones in jute bags in a well aired cool location.

Tip

Remove the flowers as they appear for the first 10 days, this will increase your yield.

Pumpkins

Sow Seeds in Greenhouse/on Windowsill: April to June
Sow Seeds Directly Outdoors: Better to start indoors
Transplant Outdoors: May to July
Depth to Plant: 2cm (3/4")
Distance Between Rows: 60cm (24")
Distance Between Plants: 60cm (24")
Harvest: September to November

A Little Bit About The Crop

Pumpkins are great to grow especially if you have children, they are also fun to look at. Every year we save the seeds from our best pumpkin. We keep them in a jar on the windowsill, let them dry out and use them the next year. Sow the seeds into rootrainers or small pots and keep them in the greenhouse or on the windowsill, until the chance of frost has passed. Plant them out in their final positions in soil with plenty of manure. One plant can produce quite a few pumpkins, but I would limit them to two pumpkins per plant in order to get the best fruit. As the pumpkins grow move them about gently so they develop a regular shape and a good skin. Keep the roots well watered. After harvesting place them on a hard surface outside to let them ripen for a few days.

Storage

If kept in a cool place, pumpkins can stay fresh for 3 - 4 weeks.

Recipe
Roast Pumpkin Seeds For Salads or Snacks

Pumpkins have loads of seeds so maybe save some for planting and roast some. Take off all the fleshy bits, run the seeds under the tap to clean them. Dry them before placing them onto a baking tray. Pour olive oil over them and then add seasoning. This can be any flavour you like, garlic, chilli, or just salt and pepper. Bake them until golden brown in a medium hot oven.

Radishes

Sow Seeds in Greenhouse/on Windowsill: No need
Sow Seeds Directly Outdoors: January to September
Depth to Plant: 1cm (1/2")
Distance Between Rows: 15cm (6") summer varieties
20cm (9") winter varieties
Distance Between Plants: Small radishes 2cm (1"), big radishes 4cm (2")
Harvest: 4 - 5 weeks after planting

A Little Bit About The Crop
You can start growing radishes all the way from the end of January under poly tunnels or cloches to September, the last harvest being in October. Radishes are a very satisfying crop to grow as they are quick and easy, but they have their limitations when it comes to eating them. Make sure that the earth has been well turned over and has plenty of compost, sow the seeds 1cm (1/2")apart. When they are growing, if they are too close just thin them out to roughly 2 - 4cm (1 - 2"). After about 4 - 5 weeks the radishes are ready for eating. The winter varieties can stay in the ground until you are ready to harvest them. There are quite a few varieties of radishes so be adventurous and choose something different.

Storage
You can store radishes like carrots either in an airy jute bag, hung in a cool room, or in a box of sand, not letting the radishes touch each other. In a jute bag the radishes should last for roughly 6 - 8 weeks.

Tip
Radishes grow well in patio planters outside the kitchen door, or in between rows of plants such as peas or carrots.

Rhubarb

Plant Crowns in Greenhouse/on Windowsill: No
Plant Crowns Directly Outdoors: February to May
Transplant Outdoors: No
Depth to Plant: Just below the surface of the soil – the right way up!
Distance Between Rows: 60cm (24")
Distance Between Plants: 60cm (24")
Harvest: April to July

A Little Bit About The Crop

You can buy rhubarb seeds but they take a lot longer to grow than already established crowns. Crowns are available in shops, or if you have a friend who has rhubarb, it may be ready to be lifted and split into pieces (sets). This should be done every five years or so. Plant your crown in well manured earth, bearing in mind that this will be your rhubarb's home for years rather than months unlike most of your vegetables. In about April the year after you have planted the crowns, you can start to pull and twist off the rhubarb stems which should be ready for eating. Never leave less than 4 stalks on the plant and finish cropping in July. If you have a well established plant you can start the season off a couple of months earlier by 'forcing' the plants. This basically means covering the plant with an upturned bucket, bin or traditional rhubarb forcer. Again don't forget to give your rhubarb a good dollop of manure once a year.

Storage

Boil the rhubarb with a little water and add some sugar. When it is soft and still piping hot, bottle it. Or you can freeze it uncooked.

Tip

Rhubarb leaves are POISONOUS, don't eat them.
Boiling rhubarb is very good for your pans, the acidity cleans them really well!

Rocket

Sow Seeds in Greenhouse/on Windowsill: March to June
Sow Seeds Directly Outdoors: June to September
Transplant Outdoors: May to September
Depth to Plant: 1cm (1/2")
Distance Between Rows: 20cm (8")
Distance Between Plants: 10cm (4")
Harvest: April to November

A Little Bit About The Crop

Rocket can either be started off in small pots on a windowsill or in the greenhouse, or it can be sown directly outside. I find that keeping the seedlings covered with a poly tunnel or a cloche during the spring and with a net or a fleece during the hotter months, helps to protect them and speed up their growth. Rocket very quickly goes to seed once it has matured, Keeping it watered well can help stall this. I sow my seeds every month to ensure a constant supply of rocket for the length of the summer.

Storage

In a plastic bag in a cool place for 2 - 4 days. Don't let the rocket get too cold or it will wilt as soon as it warms up.

Point

Rocket adds a great peppery taste to salads. It is delicious with a balsamic vinegar dressing or in a bacon butty.

Spinach

Sow Seeds in Greenhouse/on Windowsill: No
Sow Seeds Directly Outdoors: March to August
Transplant Outdoors: No
Depth to Plant: 2cm (3/4")
Distance Between Rows: 30cm (12")
Distance Between Plants: 15 - 20cm (6 - 8")
Harvest: All year round, 4 - 8 weeks after planting

A Little Bit About The Crop

Sow your spinach seeds directly outside in their final positions. Sow them in shallow lines quite thinly. Cover them with poly tunnels or cloches to protect them and to encourage growth, watch out for slugs. As the seedlings appear, thin them out to about 15 - 20cm (6 - 8") apart. You can pick the smaller more tender leaves when they are about 7cm (3")long and use them in salads, anything bigger than that should be cooked for a short amount of time and can be eaten as a hot vegetable. Keep picking the leaves so that a) they don't run to seed and b) they keep on growing. Perpetual Spinach is the spinach that I always plant as you only need to plant one lot and it lasts for months and months, sometimes even years – very easy. Perpetual spinach is not actually spinach but looks and is eaten in exactly the same way.

Storage

Not for long about 2 days in a plastic bag in the fridge.

Tip

The more you pick the more it grows.
Delicious served hot with a spoon of crème freche mixed in.

Strawberries

Plant from: Anytime when there is not a frost
Distance Between Rows: 45cm (18")
Distance Between Plants: 30cm (12")
Harvest: May to October depending on variety

A Little Bit About The Crop

Strawberries are a fruit not a vegetable, but I couldn't resist squeezing them into my book as they are such a pleasure to grow and eat! The best thing to do is to buy some strawberry plants, usually during the early Spring, and then to plant them out into well manured soil. Strawberries produce their best fruit when they are in their second and third years, so remember they will be in the same place for a good few years. During the harvesting season, you may want to protect the strawberries from rotting by placing some straw underneath, I don't seem to need to myself as my patch is fairly dry. If you don't have the space for strawberries don't forget that you can plant them in patio planters, this can be quite good as you can move them to warm spots or even encourage more fruit by placing the whole thing in a greenhouse.

Strawberries are so easy to propagate (reproduce). After the harvesting season you will notice that growing off the strawberry plant there is a shoot, with a baby strawberry plant developing on the end. When this shoot has rooted itself to the ground you can a) leave it there b) move it to a better spot c) replace an old plant with it d) give it away if you don't want it!

Beware of birds, once they find a supply of yummy ripe strawberries, they will be gone in a matter of hours. Cover them with nets as soon as they start to ripen. Also beware of slugs. They are much slower in their approach but also enjoy strawberries.

The first harvest of your strawberries will be delicious and sweet, towards the end of the season I find that they are not quite as good and this is when I collect them for jam making. Yum. When the harvest is over cut off the old leaves.

Storage

You can freeze strawberries individually on a tray, but they won't retain their texture. The best way of preserving them is to make jam.

Point

If you are short on space for growing strawberries why not buy a strawberry planter and grow them on a patio in the sunshine. Children love them and weeding is minimal.

Swedes

Sow Seeds Directly Outdoors: April to June
Depth to Plant: 1cm (1/2")
Distance Between Rows: 30cm (12")
Distance Between Plants: 22cm (9")
Harvest: September to February

A Little Bit About The Crop

I think that people regard swedes as old fashioned, and perhaps just another root vegetable.
They could be right, but I also think that a good variety of vegetables can make life a bit more fun.
Swedes are very easy to grow, so why not give it a try. The ground should be prepared as you would
for cabbages or broccoli – dig in the autumn and then later tread down the earth to make it firm.
Sow very thinly, as the seedlings appear, thin them out to 22cm (9") apart. Keep them weed free
and well watered. As usual watch out for slugs especially during the early stages.

Storage

Keep swedes as you would potatoes, in a cool room for up to a couple of months.

Point

Swedes are a must on Burns night in Scotland, it is traditionally served with haggis.
We love eating mashed swedes, cook as you would cook mashed potatoes.

Sweet corn

Sow Seeds in Greenhouse/on Windowsill: April to May
Sow Seeds Directly Outdoors: I wouldn't bother
Transplant Outdoors: May to June
Depth to Plant: 2cm (3/4")
Distance Between Rows: 45cm (18")
Distance Between Plants: 45cm (18")
Harvest: July to September

A Little Bit About The Crop

Sweet corn is another of those vegetables like peas that as soon as you pick them, they start to loose their sweetness. So pick them just before you would like to eat them. Sweet corn is one of the vegetables that children like growing as it grows fast and they can make popcorn with it in the autumn. Sweet corn are not too fussy about their soil, a bit of manure and a good forking over. They are fussier about their location. They like non windy, sunny spots. Sow the seeds into rootrainers or small 3" pots. When they are about 15 - 20cm (6 - 8") high and the frosts are no longer a risk, harden them off for a few days then plant them out 45cm (18") apart. Plant them in blocks rather than rows. This assists with pollination as they are wind pollinated. Water them well. The sweet corn is ready to pick when the juice squeezed out by a thumbnail is like watery milk.

Storage

For as little time as possible; you could of course freeze them straight away, but there isn't much point as you can buy frozen or tinned corn so cheaply. You can leave the corn on the cob until the autumn when they should have dried out a great deal. Then use the corn for popcorn. I have yet to do this!

Point

There are not many vegetables that profit from being overcooked but sweet corn is one of the ones that is better for you when well cooked. As you cook it hard and fast the levels of Ferulic acid rise, Ferulic acid is an antioxidant – antioxidants get rid of free radicals that help to cause heart disease, aging and other nasty disorders. Anything with high antioxidant levels is good for you.

Tomatoes

Sow Seeds in Greenhouse/on Windowsill: January to April
Sow Seeds Directly Outdoors: February to April
Transplant Outdoors: May to August
Depth to Plant: 1cm (1/2")
Distance Between Rows: 30cm (12")
Distance Between Plants: 20cm (8")
Harvest: July to September

A Little Bit About The Crop

Growing your own tomatoes is so satisfying, everyone who has a vegetable patch must grow them. There is nothing like the smell of the tomato plant and the taste of your own tomatoes. Successfully growing tomatoes is a little harder than you may think. There are quite a few things that can go wrong. If you have had problems with diseases such as blight in the past I would be tempted to kick the tomato plants out of the patch for a year or two and grow them in either grow bags, patio planters or pots. Sow your seeds thinly on a windowsill or in a greenhouse under a sprinkling of compost. Make sure that your patch has been well forked and manured. When the seedlings have about 5 or 6 leaves on, transplant them to 22cm (10") pots. Keep them under cover and gently watered. When they are about 30cm (12") tall plant them into their final positions. As the plants grow they will need some form of support, I use bamboo canes. Tie them on gently. They will also need to have their shoots between the main stem and the leaves pinched out. Doing this adds light, air and energy to your tomato. It doesn't mean you will get fewer tomatoes in fact you will get more and they will be better. Growing garlic and nasturtiums near your tomatoes help prevent bugs attacking. Water frequently.

Storage

A week or so in a cool place.

Tip

Cherry tomatoes are earlier to ripen than other varieties, considering England's climate, I would try these. Make green tomato chutney with any tomatoes that will not ripen.
Knowledge is knowing a tomato is a fruit; Wisdom is not putting it in a fruit salad.

Turnips

Sow Seeds Directly Outdoors: March to August
Depth to Plant: 1cm (1/2")
Distance Between Rows: 30cm (12")
Distance Between Plants: 15cm (6")
Harvest: June to October or March to April

A Little Bit About The Crop

Turnips are often grown to feed animals such as pigs. They are also allowed into the vegetable garden and are grown for the table. I believe that root vegetables and different types of squash etc are becoming popular in this day and age, especially when roasted or used in salads. Sow the seeds thinly, directly where they are to grow. As the seedlings appear, thin them out leaving one good seedling every 15cm (6") or so. Keep the plants well watered. No manure necessary here. Pull up the turnips when they are the size of a snooker ball. You can also sow the seeds in late summer, then use the leaves as they come up in March for peppery salads or as spinach. Experiment and see if you like it!

Storage

Leave in the ground over winter and pull them up as you need them or store in a cool place as you would for other root vegetables, maybe in a jute bag.

Recipe

Peel and chop the turnips into cubes about 2cm x 2cm (1" x 1"). Place them in an oven proof dish with chopped garlic, a sprinkling of salt, cumin seeds, a trickle of honey and some olive oil. Roast them until golden brown. Delicious served with roast beef. Hmmm.

Gardening Terms

Annuals	Plants that last only 1 season.
Biennials'	A plant that has a two year life cycle.
Blight	This is an infection that often affects potatoes and tomatoes, the leaves start shrivelling and grow brown blotches. Not good news. It first attacks the leaves then rapidly the rest of the plant. Cut off infected areas as soon as you detect it, this may save them.
To blanche	The boiling of vegetables for only a minute or so, then putting into cold water to stop more cooking and to keep texture. Vegetables are usually blanched before freezing.
Blown	This happens to brussels sprouts when they have been left for too long, rather like bolting.
To bolt	When a vegetable such as a lettuce starts to shoot up, loosing the texture and shape of the crop. Not good. The plant will also run to seed.
To bottle	Bottling is another way of conserving your crops. I usually blanche the vegetables for a minute and then with the water store it into storage jars, obviously putting as much vegetable in as possible. The jars need to be sealed when extremely hot to preserve the vegetables.
Brassicas	A plant group consisting of plants such as cabbages, brussels sprouts, broccoli, cauliflowers, turnips and swedes etc.
Capsicum	Another word for peppers
Chitting	This applies to seed potatoes. Leave them in the light for 2 - 6 weeks, so that shoots appear on the potatoes. These should be fat and not longer than 1cm 1/2"
Cloches	Often in the shape of a bell or tunnel, usually a clear material to encourage growth. This protects your plants from pests and weather.
Crowns	Similar to bulbs.
Cucurbits	A plant group consisting of plants such as courgettes, gourds and cucumbers.
Drills	To sow in drills, means to sow seeds in shallow lines in the earth.
Earth up	This means to pile earth up around the base of the plant as it grows. Keeping the vegetable under the earth as with asparagus or potatoes. In order to blanche the crop or to support the stem with the earth.

Forcing	Making the plants grow faster, by either depriving them of light or raising the temperature. The result is normally an earlier sweeter, more tender crop.
Harden off	When you take a plant out of the greenhouse or windowsill and let it stand for a few days in its pot outside, bringing it in at night, before planting it into its final position in the garden.
Legumes	A plant group consisting of plants such as green beans, peas etc.
Perennials	Plants that come up year after year for example, rhubarb and asparagus.
Poly Tunnels	There are different types of poly tunnels, but most of the ones mentioned in this book are of about 30-60cm (1-2ft) high and 3m (10ft) in length. You can also get larger ones rather like a greenhouse.
Propagate	To reproduce plants i.e. To grow from seeds or cuttings.
Runner	An off shoot of a plant, such as strawberries.
Sets	Mini onion bulbs are known as sets.
Solanaceae	A plant group consisting of plants such as potatoes, tomatoes and aubergines.
Spawn	Particles of wheat or millet cooked, then covered with fungi, used for growing mushrooms.
To Thin	This means to remove the smaller weaker plants in between the better ones, leaving room for the plants to grow to their full potential. If there are too many too close they won't grow properly.
To Till	To till the ground means to plough or dig it up.
Tilth	In reference to the condition of the earth, a good tilth usually means an even fine texture that is good for growing seeds in.